TIME…HEALS IN THE SPIRIT

POET AUTHENTICATOR AND AUTHOR
Ida Greenlee Cheeks

PHOTOGRAPHERS:
Ruthie B. Lee Towers
Ida B. Greenlee Cheeks
Arthur S. Cheeks, Jr.
CLIP ART ICONS

WEBSITE:
Ifox.wordpress.com

E-MAIL:
Ifoxproperties@aol.com

ISBN: 9798720110567

IMPRINT: Independently Published

BOOK AVAILIABILITY:
AMAZON Kindle Direct Publishing
www.amazon.com

TIME…HEALS IN THE SPIRIT

~ CONTENTS ~

A

Conception
    Ideation. Thought.

A

Respiration
    Breath

A

Conglomeration. Configuration. Calibration.

A

Masterpiece. Opus. Ideology.

A

Life
Came Forth
Everybody. Flora and Fauna. Everything
Abstract. Tangible.

A

Mystery
Secret
Revealed if Only We Universally Could Rationalize It All…
    Love Conquers All Not Hate

A

Plethora
    Thoughts. Words.
        Pass This Way…One Day A.M. Meridian P.M.
Good Morning. Good Afternoon. Good Evening. Good Night.
Wakeup. Sleep. Peculiarity
    Awakened State…Life is Wispily…Light Waves
    Hello. Goodbye. By-and-By in the Howdy! Howdy!

A

Train Whistle Blows Easing On Up from Down the Main Line
Borders:
Chicago Beverly Woods
Merrionette Park
Blue Island
Harvey
Riverdale
Dolton Onward…Indiana. Michigan. Canada.
As I Hear Then Singing for Inspiration:
    "This Train is Bound for Glory! Get On Board!"

AGING…ZENITHAL

…But where does the Spirit reside?

Song of Inspiration:

"Somewhere Over the Rainbow!"

We need to stop saying what our Mother (Momma) and Father (Daddy) did.

Know that we have the Free Will to Choose what "WE" do, Right or Wrong!

AGING…ZENITHAL

This is the Best Time for the Rest of Our Life.

AGING…ZENITHAL

Why is it that We have conversations?

When, everything We say, have to be always right?

AGING…ZENITHAL

Inspiration:

ECCLESIASTES 12:1-14

Am I Destroying Myself?
Grieving
Memories
Conversations
Self-Effacement to Self-Analysis
Intelligence. Stupid. Ignorant.
Me. Myself. I and Others Personification
Internal. External.
Factors
Humble…ing
Inspiration
Overcomes
Grumble…ing
Between A Rock and A Hard Place?
Dependence Meets Independence
Me. Myself. I and Others Co-Exist
Am I Destroying Myself?
Ego
Self-Worth
Emotional Energy
Outbursts…
Philosophical Indentations
Depth…
Curvature to Journey Onward Again
Me. Myself. I and Others Paths
Can Be, As Likenesses and Differences…Don't Trip! (Old School Lingo)
Inhale…Exhale
Nature Answers…Stay In Touch with Life!

Ask

"Are You Crying for Yourself or Someone Else or Something Else?"

I Ask Myself.

"You Are Just Like a Door, Swings Open and Close…"

I Ask Then Answer Myself.

"What Is That To You?"

I Ask Then Reflect Myself.

"Go Seek Intrinsic Wisdom, Knowledge, Understanding and Commonsense."

I Heard in My Dream, Arthur's Voice.

"TIME HEALS."

BOUNT(Y)IFULNESS

As I look out the south windowpane
The Cardinal
I see him dressed in his entire highlighted splendor
So, near here
As usual
Spring Time Acknowledgment
BOUNTIFULNESS
Certainly, They Understand…
The Cardinal
She is not far
Arrayed the same
I will hear her before now soon…
Seeking then found nourishment
As He then She Before Now Always
Perched high or low
Nature Essence and Presence Ethereal Substantiated Sustained
Singing. Chirping. Scratching. Pecking. Feeding.
Melodiously Inspiration
Standing On the Multitudinous Promises…
Words of Recognition
BOUNT(Y)IFULNESS
I Read Before Again Now for Elaboration to Share…
1 Kings 10
2 Corinthians 9
BOUNT(Y)IFULNESS
I Believe!
Sense
BOUNTIFULNESS

Empty Reflections
Ideation
Mirrored Adjudication Face-to-Face Faces
Me. Myself. I. You and Us…

Empty Reflections
Ideation
Written to Be…
Respiration
Thought
Word
Aspiration
Agitation
Inspiration
Action
Reaction
Revelation
Transformation
Acknowledgment
Application
Assimilation
Actualization
Adaptation
Reverence
Articulation
Coherence
Generational
Acclimation
Translated
Life Spoken So, It Is Being…
2 Corinthians 3:18

Empty Reflections
Ideation
Queries then Answers
Me. Myself. I. You and Us…
Who. What. When. Where. Why. How?
Synoptic…Illumination
Optimism. Pessimism. Appreciation. Condescension.

Empty Reflections
Colossians 1:12-13

I____

D____

E____

A____

T____

I____

O____

N____

Exception

Nothing
Is
Erased?
…

Brokenness
Shatters
The Happiness
Window
Forgiveness
Mends
As
Time Heals?
…

Even an Evil Lie Needs a Rest?
…

Trees Need a Bath Too?
My Uncle Clyde Stated
I Too Understand the Visualization Nature Nourishment Indication
…

Truth?
To Speak To the Ignorance
…

It
We
Just Change Form?
…

Exception
To The Rule of Dissemination?
The Book of Life Historicity
Encapsulate Many Genre Ideologies
Interpretive. Inspirative. Imperative. Live Abundantly and Infinitely

"FORGIVE"
I hear in my innerness…
Others and Myself
12.28.2020
I read
As I just completed a text…
Symbolically

Release
Increase
"FORGIVE"
2020 is slowly drifting towards the horizon.

However, 01.01.2021 is at the Surface for Beginning.
Be Blessed, Safe and Holistic with Peace, Joy, Faith and Love…
GOD'S Will Is Awesome Reverence!
And Then?
1950 ~ 1969

And Then?
1970
And Then?
1972
And Then?
1973 ~ 2019
And Then?
2020
And Then?
Facets
Like Faces and Flaws in Gemstones
Polished to Perfection and Aesthetically…
Others and Myself
"FORGIVE"
Let My Life Speak for Itself…
I Am Thankful!
And Then?
2021
Is Right There…
Celebratory for Life

See. Speak. Hear. Feel. Taste. Sense
The Encapsulated Experiences Acknowledged…
Breathe the Breath of Life
"FORGIVE"

GET

When They are Trying to GET What You've Got…

They Can No Longer GET What You've Got…

Because

You Will not Give Them What You've Got to Get…

Spirit
Soul
Heart
Mind
Intellect
Emotion
Body
Being
Economics
Conversations
Laugh Out Loud
Teary-Eyed
Spasmodic
Moments

So, When We All GET Together Again and Got What We Got to GET…

We'll All Be Better and Happier to GET Together With What We've Got

The Got Becomes a Shared Got to GET…

We Have to GET Ourselves Together to Make Sense Too of What We Got to

GET

What I Have and You Have Then Got Shared Eventually…Interrelatedness.

I Recollect It To Be…
We
Can
All

Run
Walk
Skip
Hop
Jump
Slide
Reside
Leave
Rest
Coincide
Confide
Lay Down Our Dispositional Burden. Pick Up Our Dispensational Victory.
Beside Lie. Sit. Stoop. Stand On or In or Over or Through
A
Hole

But
We Can't Jive Connive Criticize Always Peep and Hide

From
Ourselves
That is a certainty…

Facing the Truth
As
I Recollect It To Be….

I Will…

    Wake Up
    Make Up My Mind
    Take Sometime to Unwind
    Fake Not Intentions for Selfish-Gratification
        Find the Kind of Life to Live
    Intake a Breath
        Wind to Breathe
    Sake of and My Self of for GOD'S Will to Be Done

I Will…

    Wake Up
    Forsake Not the Word of Life
               Strife Will come, If I Do Too
        Have My…
    Cake and Eat It Too
        For Greed. Ambition. Selfish. Pleasure. Fame. Force…
        By Any Means
        I Shall Not
        However, Because in Time…

I Will…

    Wake Up
        Entitled to Everybody and Everything for GOD'S Will Is…
        Not Spreading Venomous Thoughts. Words. Action.
        However, An Antidote…
        Holistic
        I Heard the Robin's Song Today…Confirmation
    Take a Stand on the Promises
        The Cardinal Came Too…Singing Melodiously!
        The Snow Bird Too…Perched On the Shrubbery Limb
    Stake Out from Their Journey for Their Territory…
        Sing Spring Certainly is On Its Way, Just Around the Corner!
I Will…Wake Up
        Shake Off the Old for the New Being
        Take within My Soul Liberation…Grace Acknowledged
        Quake to Assurance Exhilarate…
        Raise My Voice for the Gloriousness!
        See the Manifestation and Promises to Behold…Praise
        A New Day. Weeks. Months. Years to Come…AMEN!

It
May Be at My House
Today

And

Your House
Tomorrow

And

Somebody Else's House
Yesterday

But…And

It
Will be
One Day…Anyway
AMEN, TRUTH.

PROVERBS 3:3-4
"Let Not Mercy and Truth Forsake Thee:
Bind Them About Thy Neck;
Write Them Upon the Table of Thine Heart:
So Shalt Thou Find Favor and Good Understanding
In the Sight of GOD and People."

"I know You…! I'm Learning."
Looking at the Pictures…
Depth
Like Primed Water from a Prism Shimmered Well
Consciousness
Becomes
A
Saturation Point
Of
Recollection and Recognition…

Life

Took

Me

And

Rolled

Me

Like

A

Lint Ball…

Stitching

February 2020 ~ 2013 February

Backward!

OLD SOUL

They Have

An

OLD SOUL

But

Slick Ways…

Chance to Change Though

To

GOD

Be the Glory…

Manifested

On the Edge

Living
On the Edge
Of
Consciousness
Life
Ebbs and Flows
As
Tides
Timeliness
Of the Ocean…
Resurgence
Onto the Shoreline
Energy
Waves
Celestially
Terrestrially
Aquatically
Rough
Plus
Serene
Humankind
Flora
Fauna
Essence
Presence
Scenes to Meditate
Coherence
Living
On the Edge
Of
Consciousness
Life
Ebbs and Flows
As
Tides
Timeliness
Of the Ocean…

Renaissance
Past
Present
Future
Mediate
Cathartically
Decisions to Construe…
Living
On the Edge
Of
Consciousness
Life
Ebbs and Flows
As
Tides
Timeliness
Of the Ocean…
Concurrence
Heartily
Live. Laugh. Love Life with Passion and Purpose
Gratefulness
As
Sea Turtles
Portrayal
I Shall to Be
Seeking. Knocking. Opening Doors to the Beauty…
Rhythmically
Living
On the Edge
Of
Consciousness
Life
Ebbs and Flows
As Tides
Timeliness
Of the Ocean…
Sustenance
Sustainability
So, It Is To Be, AMEN.

One Prevails!

Truth

Lie

Go Figure Mentation

Lamentation

Celebration

Mind

Divine

Sublime

Ridiculous

Time

On

Off

Proliferate

Indicative

Inspirative

Disheartened

Construe

Misconstrue

Configuration…

One Prevails!

People

Why do We…Us People think We are such a genius and others are not?

However, don't We have the same characteristics?

Stretched to the limit of fraying

Like fabrics
Of
Fallibility to Infallibility

For our Telomeres
To
Rewire
Restring
Hiding
Sliding
Conniving
Confiding

People

Healing to Be Functional Citizens and Caretakers of Our Universe
Celestial
Terrestrial
Aquatic

People

This Is It for Now and Generational Subduing in Our Explorations!

Genesis 1:26-31

Rain…Sunday Came

When Rain Came

To Wash the Earth Clean…

Me Too…

I Look Out the Window Pane

West to Encapsulate

The Weatherman's Predictive

Saturday Evening Mention…

Sunday Came

As Usual…

Wet Rain Came

Precipitately

Picturesquely

Remnant of the Scenery

I Share

I Am Thankful Dear GOD…

By the Way, AMEN!

Scripted Letters

A Highlighted Thought
In
My Dreams
On
A Page
Of
Scripted Letters…
Sentence…

I Then Am Awakened
To the Coherent Intention
As Inspiration…
Remembrances
I am Thankful…
AMEN.

SASH

Y

N

ENERGY

R

G

SCENERY

A

S

WHEAT

TARES

Y

SIFTED

N

GRACEFULLY

S O

U & ME...

SYNERGY 

Tell the Conversationalist the "SOMETIMES"

Well, Martha had to find someone (Not Mary) outside her house to help her.
I asked the Conversationalist,
Is that what I needed to do?

Tell the Conversationalist the "SOMETIMES"
Do you really HATE me that much?
LOVE or HATE is a CHOICE…
A Turning Point Scenario Again?
Is this what is meant by the "SOMETIMES"?

Tell the Conversationalist the "SOMETIMES"
ABSORPTION
Sieved
Negativism or Optimism
ABSORPTION SPECTRUM
Scientific or Instinctive
Darkness Pattern Observation Exist for Dispersing Light Proliferation
Utilization
Spectroscope
Stethoscope
Prescient
Hindsight
Para Science
Parapsychology
Psychology
Realism
SCOPE
Definitive Principles to Phenomena to Live By

Tell the Conversationalist the "SOMETIMES"
Some Timed. Old Timed. All Timed. Real Timed. Authentic. Realized…
Inspiration
Ezekiel 37
Luke 10:38-42
Ephesians 5:17
John 21:21-22
John 3
Romans 12
Philippians 2

The Link
Well, I guess The Link to Us has been broken…Goodbye?
The Link
Physically…
Looking Out the East Window ReViewing the Christmas Scenery...
I Think…How do you (I) find another purpose?
Grandmother Arie. Mother Ruthie. Son Arthur…Gone!
The Link
Spiritually…
We Will Always Be Connected…Hello?.!
I Twinkle…As You, Love Stars Energy Bound Galactic Halo Outside Inside
The Link
I Sink…Intellectually. Emotionally. Philosophically. Physiologically.
The Treasured Thoughts within my Heart's Depth…Always.
The Link
Commonsensical…
I Ink…the Parchment Surfaces for the Purpose
Live. Laugh. Love Life with Passion and Purpose
The Link
Rhythmically…
I Wink…Eye-to-Eye as Life Circadian Acknowledgement
The Link
Holistically…
I Crinkle…Crackle Senses as Sun Rays Dream Realm Enlighten Perpetuity
Proliferated Attuned Orchestrated Symphonic Symbiosis!

THE MASTER…THE TEACHER
"I"
Said, HE…
Who is the Subject and Object of "I" of Them, Which Wrote the Book?
Through You for You for Us…Inspirational
THE MASTER…THE TEACHER
"I"

THE WORD. THE LOGOS.
Who is the Incarnate Being of the "I AM THAT I AM"?

El Shaddai	Lord God almighty
El Elyon	The Most High God
Adonai	Lord, master
Yaweh	Lord, Jehovah
Jehovah Nissi	The Lord My Banner
Jehovah-Raah	The Lord My Supplier
Jehovah Rapha	The Lord that Heals
Jehovah Shammah	The Lord is There
Jehovah Tsidkenu	The Lord Our Righteousness
Jehovah Mekoddishkem	The Lord Who Sanctifies You
El Olam	The Everlasting God
Elohim	God
Qanna	Jealous
Jehovah Jireh	The Lord Will Provide
Jehovah Shalom	The Lord is Peace
Jehovah Sabaoth	The Lord of Hosts

THE MASTER…THE TEACHER
"I"
Created and Purposed You, You and You All…Mysteries?
Personifications
Logotherapy?
Universally
Dispersions
Dispensational
Seeds. Planted. Watered. Harvested.
A Life to Live the Blessings to Behold
Encouraged. Shared. Sustained. Holistically
People. Flora. Fauna. Everything Imaginable. Celestial. Terrestrial. Aquatic.
THE MASTER…THE TEACHER
"I"
Set in Order "In the Beginning God Created…" The WORD. The LOGOS.

THIS PACKAGE
Awakened Consciously Cathartic

THIS PACKAGE
Awakened
The Depth of Mysteries and Enlightenment
Wisdom. Knowledge. Understanding. Commonsensical.

THIS PACKAGE
Consciously
Redemption
Teaches

THIS PACKAGE
Cathartic
Wholly By GOD
A Person
By Blood
By Power
CHRIST Redeems the Believer from Guilt and Penalty of Sin
The HOLY SPIRIT Delivers from the Dominion of Sin
(I Surmise Reasoning Sin is Trouble. Adversity. Misfortune.)

THIS PACKAGE
Matthew 5; 15
Luke 5; 16
John 5; 12; 15
Romans 8
Ephesians 2
1 Corinthians 15
Hebrews 1
Revelation 20; 21

THIS PACKAGE
Awakened Consciously Cathartic

TIME?
FORM
Who
What
When
Where
Why
How?

TIME?
HEARD
Running
From The TRUTH…
Running
To The TRUTH…
Running
On The TRUTH….
Running
In The TRUTH…
Running
For The TRUTH…
Running
Beside The TRUTH…
Running
Becomes The TRUTH…
Running
Paths to Reside Around Those Queries for TRUTH…
Running
Answers to Respire Come Out Eventually as The TRUTH…
Running. Run.ning. Run.n.ing. Run Into a Respite Finally for The TRUTH!

TIME?
SEEN
Veiled or Visible
On or Off the Hour Glass Sand Calibration to Clock Synchronization
One Way or the Other Way…
Another Way Surfaces
Somebody or Something
Somewhere or No Where
Far or Near…To or In or Through…For or Here…From or There

TIME?
STANDING
On the Promises
THE WORD
THE LOGOS
GENRES
Wisdom. Knowledge. Understanding. Commonsense. Deciphering…

TIME?
TALKING
Configuration then Encapsulation for Actualization
Wisdom. Knowledge. Understand. Commonsense…Proliferation
Construed the Eschewed Coherence Repetition Ingenuity Integrity

TIME?
WALKING
Essence and Presence Personified Reality is Abstract or Tangible…
Function from the Injunction Conjunction to Adjudication
READ TO READ!

TIME?
SENSE
TIME AFTER TIME
SEEKING
Self, Others, or Something
Adventure
Balance
Excitement
Humor or Sadness
GOD or Deities
History
Judgment
Purpose and Worth
Right or Wrong? The Word? The Logos? Logotherapy? Depth Psychology?
Spiritual? Sacred? Secular? Agnostic? Atheistic? Staunchness…
FAILURE or ATTAINMENT
INTERFACE
Reiteration. Relegation. Releasing. Relentlessness. Residuals…Resoluteness
Spirit. Physical. Emotion. Cultural. Kindred. Social. Economics. Ecology.

TIME?
BEING
REVELATIONAL
ASSIMILATION
LIE or TRUTH
ACKNOWLEDGMENT
CATHARTIC
PEACE. JOY. FAITH. HOPE. LOVE ABIDES…SUSTAINING GRACE
ALWAYS RIGHT ON TIME, THANKFUL!

TIME…HEALS IN THE SPIRIT
> Seals. Reveals Conceals. Bondages Inherent Releases …
>> Steals Away in the Midnight Hour
>> Look? Crook of the Shepherd. Rod of Power…Duty. Authority.

TIME…HEALS IN THE SPIRIT
> Seals. Reveals Conceals. Bondages Inherent Releases …
>> Intermingles
>> Tingles
>>> Tickles. Laughter. Sorrow.
>>> Nerve Endings…Telomeres Fray Mend Again Protection

TIME…HEALS IN THE SPIRIT
> Seals. Reveals Conceals. Bondages Inherent Releases …
>> Cringles
>>> Sail Onto Rope Rings Secure in the Winds of Life
>> Crinkles. Crumples. Redesigned. Transformative.

TIME…HEALS IN THE SPIRIT
> Seals. Reveals Conceals. Bondages Inherent Releases …
>> Crumbles
>>> Diminishes
>>> Stretches. Draws Out. Drawn In. Straightens Out…
>> Stumbles. Mumbles. Articulate.
>>> Eventually

TIME…HEALS IN THE SPIRIT
> Seals. Reveals Conceals. Bondages Inherent Releases …
>> Co-Mingles
>>> Acknowledged
>>> Prevails…Inhales and Exhales Sustaining Life
>>> Evidently

TIME…HEALS IN THE SPIRIT
> Seals. Reveals Conceals. Bondages Inherent Releases …
>> Circumspect
>> Circumvent
>> Vent
>>> Chimney Top Reshape Elemental Combustion
>>> As Mindscape Escape Breaths into the Ether

TIME…HEALS IN THE SPIRIT

> Seals. Reveals Conceals. Bondages Inherent Releases …
>> "TIME HEALS"
>> I Heard to Think To Do? I Shared the Thought!
>> Sense…Finally, Said to Me. Myself. I to You and Us…Says, IT!
>> Well? "Get On Up and Live." Said, I did, Not Hesitatingly…
>> Recognizably

TIME…HEALS IN THE SPIRIT

> Seals. Reveals Conceals. Bondages Inherent Releases …
>> Circadian
>> Truncating
>> Replenish. Refreshing. Transcending.
>>> Keys Open…Power. Used Wisely.

TIME…HEALS IN THE SPIRIT

> Seals. Reveals Conceals. Bondages Inherent Releases …
>> Are On Our Side. Inside. Outside. Reside. Below. Above.
>>> Physiological
>>> Psychological
>>> Intellectual Emotional See Hear Speak Taste Touch Sense
>>> Philosophical
>>> Cultural
>>> Ecological
>>> Economics

TIME…HEALS IN THE SPIRIT

> Seals. Reveals Conceals. Bondages Inherent Releases …
>>> In the Now By-and-By One Way or Another Way
>>> Whether We Are…Selectively
>>>> Indoctrinated vis-à-vis Ideologies
>>> Spiritual. Sacred. Religious. Agnostic. Atheist. Adamant.
>>> Alive or Demise…
>>>> War or Peace Surfaces in Life…Certainly
>>> Manifested Libelous Slanderous Lie or Bona Fide Truth?
>>> Live. Laugh. Love. Life Passion Purpose Journey Inspired!

TIME…HEALS IN THE SPIRIT

>> Seals. Reveals Conceals. Bondages Inherent Releases …
>>> I Am Thankful for Everybody and Everything…Holistic.
>>> So, It Is To Be…AMEN!

TRAIN TRACKS?
WELL, THEN…

STOP. LOOK. LISTEN. GO.

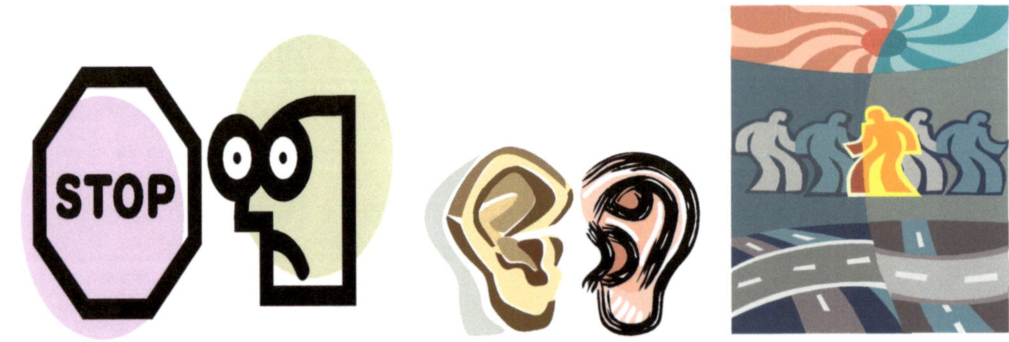

SINGING JUBILANTLY

"THIS TRAIN IS BOUND FOR GLORY…"
MANIFESTING GOD!
TRAIN TRACKS?

RATTLE TATTLE CHATTER EXIST SW…ISH SW…ISH SW…ISHING
SACRED SILENCE EASINESS
WAITING…THANKFUL!
SUSTAINING GRACE WITH HUMBLED REVERENCE
PROMISES. PATIENCE. PEACE. JOY. FAITH. KIND. LOVE. POWER.
TRIUMPHANT…SOUND ESSENCE PRESENCE!

UNDERSTAND IT

I UNDERSTAND Better to Be in the World But Not of IT.

Shenanigan

Greed
Ambition
Selfish
Pleasure
Fame
Force

Proliferation

Scientific
Cultural
Outwardly
Religious
Elegant

Observation

News Worthy
Audible
Visuals
Lie or Truth

Consequence

Sometimes, UNDERSTAND You Have to Walk Away From IT…Problem
People
Demeanor
Material Things
Ideation
Situation
Conflict
Complication

Confirmation

UNDERSTAND IT Can Only Get Better After Awhile…Solution
Life Empowerment. Time. Space. Distance.

Walking and Talking At the Same Time…W. A. I. T.

Walking

And

Talking

At

The

Same

Time…

Just won't get it

But

W. A. I. T.

Anticipatorily

Immanuel's

Transcendentness

Will

Be

Done…

Thinking About It

The Deed to Succeed…

Might Fail But Try Again

If It's All Right…

Don't Delay

Say

I'll Try

And

Make It Anyway

If Possible…

Walking

And

Talking

At

The

Same

Time…

Concentration

Inspiration

W. A. I. T.

Accepting

Immanuel's

Time

WANT (!) A MIND…A BLANK SLATE!

**What in the World Does One or Many People
WANT (!)
From Someone or Anything?
A MIND…**

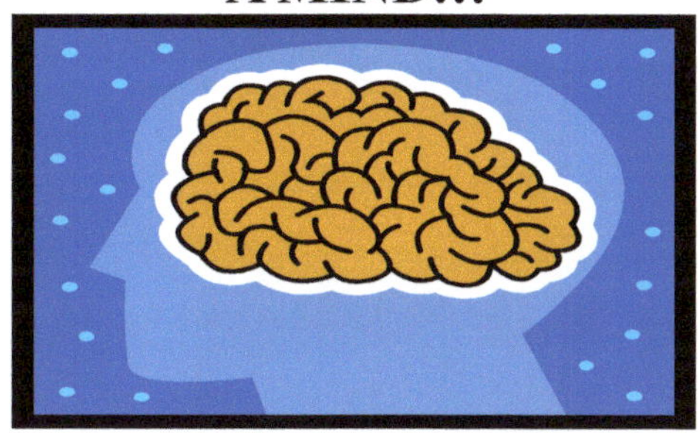

A BLANK SLATE!

**A Refuse to Give an Answer…
Thoughts. Visualizations. Spoken Words. Memories Continue Unshared**

**Go Back to Sleep…
Reaching Out…
I Awakened from the Audible Dream…
"There's Power in the Holy Spirit! There's Power in the Holy Spirit!"
I Want that Assurance.**

Why I Cry, Try to Understand

Why, GOD Took My Love Ones, Left Us By Ourselves?

I Hear the Train Whistles, Again, This A.M…

Far but Distance, It Is In…

"Just Don't Go in the Path of Destruction."

I Recognize to Be Said to Me…

Thinking…

12.23.2020

The Train Whistles Whishes By

AMEN!

All Through the Night, Awakening, Still, I Hear…

The Distance but Near…Solitude

AMEN!

Zealous Worship Time

Memories Proliferate Negatives to Positives Mediate Uplifts Visualizations

Somebody's Always Trying to Keep Somebody Else On~Off or In~Out Of
Genres of Historical Data
Establishments
Home
Family Lineage. Neighbors.
Church
Hospitals
Schools. Universities.
Institutions
Entertainment
Business…
Nature Natural Wonders to Behold Forests Parks Camping Sites
Treks On In Off the Roads of Life Lies and Truths Proliferate Transform
People. Flora. Fauna Are the Universal Essence and Presence…
Etc. etc. etc to e.g. to i.e.
Local. State. Federal. Universal Dispensation Reclamation
Whomever. Whatever. Whenever. Whys and Wherefores. However…
Fear Entanglement Enablement Imprisonment Are Attacks
Bravery Freedom Liberty Justice Empowerment Are Counterattacks
Fall. Get Up. Stand On the Promises…Acknowledgment
Love. Faith. Hope. Joy. Sustained Holistically Coherent
Spirit. Soul. Body.

🔔 **Being. Purpose. Grace.**

2 Timothy 1:9
"Who saved us and called us with a holy calling, not according to our works but according to his own purpose and grace. This grace was given to us in Christ Jesus before the ages began."

🔔 **Zealous Worship Time**

John 1:17-18
"For the law was given by Moses, but grace and truth came by Jesus Christ. No man has seen God at any time; the only begotten Son, which is in the bosom of the Father, he hath declared him."

John 4:23-24
"But the hour cometh, and now is, when the true worshippers shall worship the Father in spirit and in truth: for the Father seeketh such to worship him. God is a Spirit: and they that worship him must worship him in spirit and in truth."

2 Corinthians 3:13-18
"And not as Moses, which put a veil over his face, that the children of Israel could not steadfastly look to the end of that which is abolished: But their minds were blinded: for until this day remained the same veil untaken away in the reading of the Old Testament.; which veil done away in Christ. But even unto this day, when Moses is read, the veil is upon their heart. Nevertheless when it shall turn to the Lord Jehovah, the veil shall be taken away. Now the Lord is that Spirit: and where the Spirit of the Lord is, there is liberty. But we all, with open face (unveiled) beholding as in a glass the glory of the Lord Jehovah, are changed (transformed) into the same image from glory to glory, even as by the Spirit of the Lord."

2 Corinthians 4:13, 18
"We having the same spirit (Holy Spirit) of faith, according as it is written, I believed and therefore have I spoken; we also believe, and therefore speak…While we look not at the things which are seen, but at the things which are not seen: for the things which are seen are temporal; but the things which are not seen are eternal."

Galatians 5:1-26
"(8) Such persuasion does not come from the one who calls you…(14-15)

For the whole law is summed up in a single commandment, 'You shall love your neighbor as yourself.' If, however, you bite and devour one another, take care that you are not consumed by one another."

2 Peter 1:20-21

"First of all you must understand this, that no prophecy of scripture is a matter of one's own interpretation, because no prophecy ever came by human will, but men and women moved by the Holy Spirit spoke from God."

🔔 Zealous Temperament

Acts 21:20

"When they heard it, they praised God. Then they said to him, 'You see, brother, how many thousands of believers there are among the Jews, and they are all zealous for the law."

1 Corinthians 14:12

"So with yourselves; since you are eager for spiritual gifts, strive to excel in them for building up the church."

Titus 2:14

"He it is who gave himself for us that he might redeem us from all iniquity and purify for himself a people of his own who are zealous for good deeds."

Revelation 3:19

"I reprove and discipline those whom I love. Be earnest, therefore, and repent."

🔔 Worship Inspirational

Psalm 99:5

"Extol the LORD our God; worship at his footstool. Holy is he!"

Acts 17:23

"For as I went through the city and looked carefully at the objects of your worship, I found among them an altar with the inscription. 'To an unknown god.' What therefore you worship as unknown, this I proclaim to you."

Revelation 4:9-11

"And whenever the living creatures give glory and honor and thanks to the one who is seated on the throne, who lives forever and ever, the twenty-four elders fall before the one who is seated on the throne and worship the one who lives forever and ever; they cast their crowns before the throne, singing, 'You are worthy, our Lord and God, to receive glory and honor and power, for you created all things, and by your will they existed and were created."

🔔 Time Essentialness

Psalm 69:13
"But as for me, my prayer is unto thee, O LORD, in an acceptable time: O God, in the multitude of thy mercy hear me, in the truth of thy salvation."

Isaiah 27:12-13
"On that day the LORD will thresh from the channel of the Euphrates to the Wadi of Egypt, and you will be gathered one by one, O people of Israel. And on that day a great trumpet will be blown, and those who were lost in the land of Assyria and those who were driven out to the land of Egypt will come and worship the LORD on the holy mountain at Jerusalem."

Ecclesiastes 3:1-8
"(1) For everything there is a season, and a time for every matter under the heaven…"

Matthew 16:3
""And in the morning, 'It will be stormy today, for the sky is red and threatening.' You know how to interpret the appearance of the sky, but you cannot interpret the signs of the times."

John 4:20
"Our ancestors worshiped on this mountain, but you say that the place where people must worship is in Jerusalem."

Romans 1:24-32
"(24) Therefore God gave them up in the lusts of their hearts to impurity, to the degrading of their bodies among themselves, (24) because they exchanged the truth about God for a lie and worshiped and served the creature rather than the Creator, who is blessed forever! Amen."

Romans 13:11
"Besides this, you know what time it is, how it is now the moment for you

to wake from sleep. For salvation is nearer to us now than when we became believers.”

1 Corinthians 14:25
“After the secrets of the unbeliever’s hear are disclosed, that person will bow down before God and worship him, declaring, ‘God is really among us.’”

Hebrews 1:6-7
“And again, when he brings the firstborn into the world, he says, ‘Let all God’s angels worship him.’ Of the angels he says, ‘He makes his angels winds, and his servants flames of fire.’”

Revelation 1:1-20
“(3) Blessed is the one who reads aloud the words of the prophecy, and blessed are those who hear and who keep what is written in it; for the time is near.”

Revelation 10:6-12
“And swore by him who lives forever and ever, who created heaven and what is in it, the earth and what is in it, the sea and what is in it: ‘There will be no more delay.’”

Psalm 129:8
“The blessing of the Lord be upon you.”

“Let nothing disturb you.
Let nothing frighten you.
All things are changing.
God alone is changeless.
Patience attains the good.
One who has God lacks nothing.
God alone fills all our needs.”
~ St. Teresa of Avila

“Silence has so much meaning.”
~ Yurok

🔔 Zealous Worship Time